NATIONAL GEOGRAPHIC

Ladders

LEND ME A PAW

GENRE Social Studies Article

Read to find out about traits and instincts of working animals.

Animals Can!

by Sara Hellwege

It's a busy day in the city. One worker patrols a park to keep it safe while another leads a blind person down a sidewalk. In a nearby hospital, a third worker helps a patient recover from an illness. What do the workers have in common? They all have four legs and fur! Animals help people do many different kinds of work.

Therapy Animals

For many people, a friendly animal brings out a smile. That's the idea behind animal **therapy.** Therapy is something that heals or helps people feel better, and therapy animals are animals that help people feel better. In a typical situation, a therapy dog and its owner visit a hospital or a nursing home. In many cases, patients' moods improve around the joyful wag of the dog's tail, and patients who are anxious feel soothed when they pet its soft fur. Cats, rabbits, birds, and horses are also used as therapy animals.

A therapy horse visits senior citizens.

An animal needs the right **traits** to be a therapy animal. A trait is a quality that makes one thing different from another. Friendliness is a good trait for a therapy animal. Many dogs have this trait, and this is one reason dogs are the most common therapy animal. Other traits of good therapy animals are listed below.

Traits of Therapy Animals

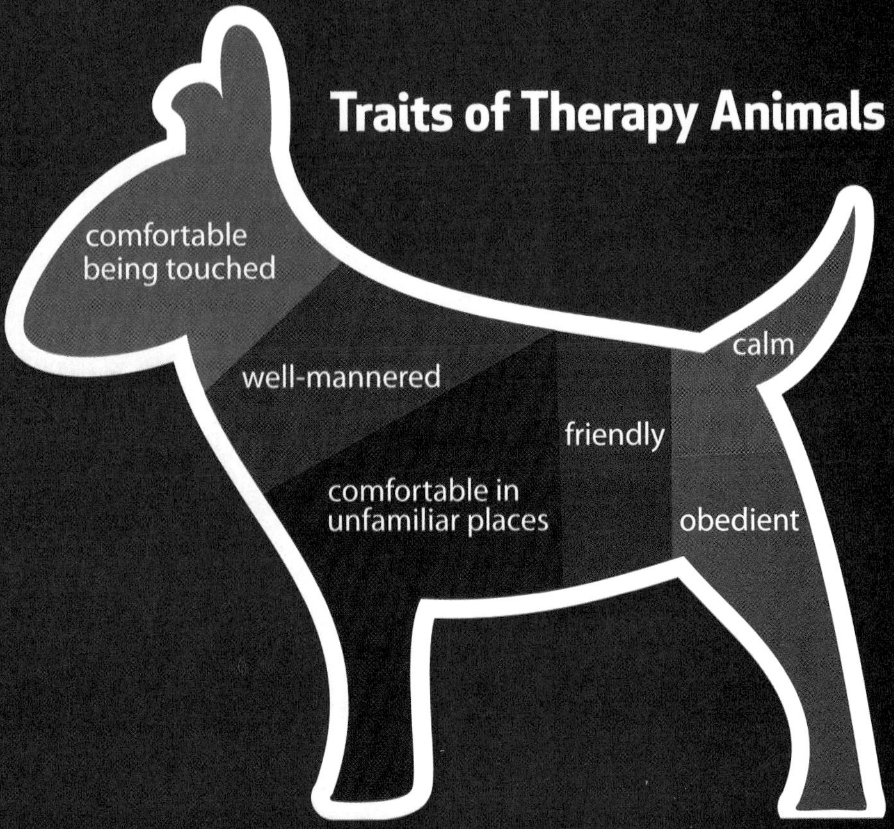

WORKING DOGS

GOLDEN RETRIEVER
Job: search and rescue dog
Traits: keen sense of smell

Working Dogs

Some animals work for a living. In addition to traits, **instincts** are important for working animals. An instinct is a natural ability, and animals with certain instincts are good for certain jobs. Let's take a look at dogs. Some breeds have an instinct to herd, some to hunt, and some to protect. Because of their instincts, certain jobs come naturally to certain breeds of dogs.

Herding dogs have an instinct to gather and move livestock, such as cattle and sheep. They may even try to herd people if there are no livestock around! In order to do their job well, herd dogs need to be trained. They are taught **commands** that include words, whistles, and hand signals.

Search and rescue dogs rely on their instinct to hunt in order to find people who are missing or trapped. A keen sense of smell is a trait that helps them do this. The dogs also go through extensive training during which they follow a human scent, learn commands, and get rewards. Then they're ready to work in emergency situations. For example, after an earthquake or avalanche they go through rubble or snow, searching for victims who are trapped.

Guard dogs rely on their instinct to protect in order to keep people, places, and livestock safe. Strength and a loud, mean bark are important traits that guard dogs use to do their job. They are trained to use these instincts and traits to alert their owners and scare away intruders.

BORDER COLLIE
Job: herd dog
Traits: nimble, loud bark

GERMAN SHEPHERD
Job: guard dog
Traits: strong, stern bark

Service Animals

When you hear the word ***service***, you might think of ***help***, and that's exactly what service animals do. A service animal is a dog that's trained to help a person with a **disability.**

- Guide dogs are service animals that help people who are blind get safely from place to place.
- Hearing dogs are service animals that help people who are deaf. They are trained to alert their owners to sounds, such as a ringing doorbell, and to lead them to the sound.
- Assistance dogs are service animals that help people with physical disabilities. For example, they may pull someone in a wheelchair, pick up dropped items, or open doors.

SERVICE ANIMALS

According to U.S. law, service animals are permitted in public places, such as restaurants and stores. This law is important because it gives service animals rights that other animals, such as pets, don't have. Service animals are not considered pets. They are working animals, and when they are on duty they wear a harness and a vest. If you see a guide dog or another service animal, you should follow a few simple rules:

- Talk to the person, not to the dog.
- Don't pet the dog unless you get permission. The dog is on duty and petting or talking to it can distract it from its job.

LABRADOR RETRIEVER
Job: assistance dog
Traits: nimble, strong, instinctively helpful, intelligent

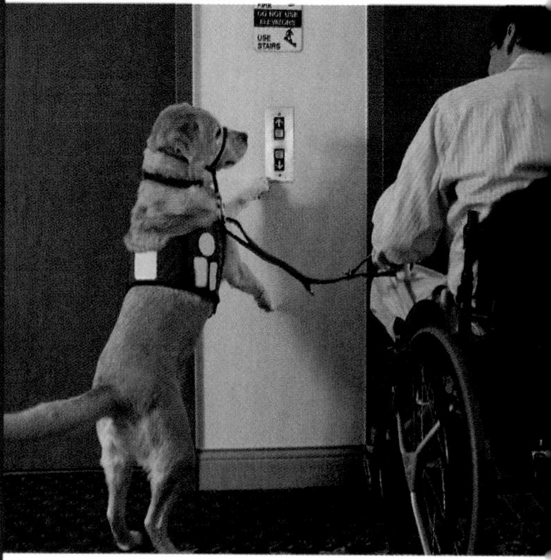

TERRIER
Job: hearing dog
Traits: alert, energetic, intelligent

LABRADOR RETRIEVER
Job: guide dog
Traits: calm, not easily distracted, intelligent

Beasts of Burden

When there's heavy work to do, a beast of burden can do the job. A pack animal carries loads, a draft animal pulls loads, and some animals do both.

In the past, people used animals to do work because there was no other option. Today, animals are used if motor vehicles are not practical or available. In different parts of the world, there are different beasts of burden, including donkeys, oxen, water buffalo, reindeer, llamas, horses, elephants, and camels. Let's take a look at a few.

Asian elephants used to work in the timber industry to clear land and carry logs in Southeast Asia. In many of these countries, logging is now illegal. Some elephants and their handlers now patrol forests to protect them from people who continue to cut down trees.

In the Andes Mountains, llamas have transported goods for centuries. They still work as pack animals in remote areas where it is difficult to use cars and other vehicles.

Camels are known as "ships of the desert." They carry heavy loads and walk up to 25 miles (40 kilometers) a day with little food and water.

The next time you see a furry, four-legged worker, remember that people and the vehicles we create can't do everything . . . and say *thanks!*

An elephant moves a fallen tree in Thailand after the tsunami in 2004.

LLAMA

Job: pack animal

Traits: sure-footed in rocky, mountainous terrain

Location: Andes Mountains, South America

ASIAN ELEPHANT

Job: pack animal and draft animal
Traits: strong, intelligent, flexible trunk
Location: India and Southeast Asia

BEASTS OF BURDEN

DROMEDARY CAMEL

Job: pack animal and draft animal
Traits: adapted for long-distance desert travel
Location: Northern Africa and the Middle East

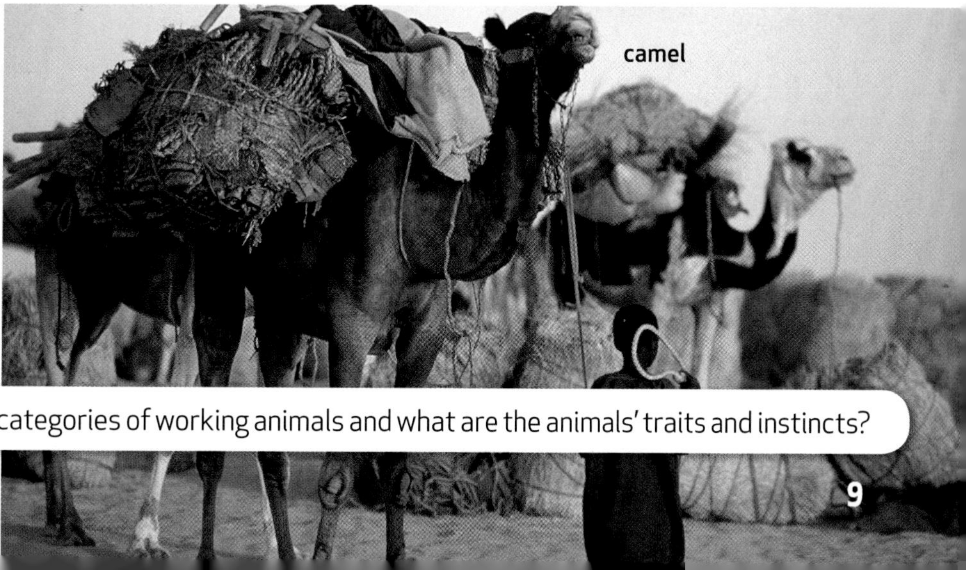

Check In What are some categories of working animals and what are the animals' traits and instincts?

GENRE Opinion Piece

Read to find out why dolphins and sea lions are used in this program instead of people.

The Navy Marine Mammal Program

by Shannae Wilson

The U.S. military has a program called the "Navy **Marine Mammal** Program." In the program, bottlenose dolphins and California sea lions participate in military operations. These marine mammals have unique **traits** that allow them to perform certain underwater tasks better than people or equipment can.

Sea lions have exceptional hearing and vision under water.

Sea lions and dolphins are excellent divers. They can dive deeper, more often, and stay under water longer than people can.

The animals follow **commands** to perform a variety of tasks. They protect ports, ships, and submarines against attacks from enemy swimmers. They also locate objects, including expensive training equipment and sea mines. A sea mine is a weapon, like an underwater bomb. After the animals locate the objects, the Navy can remove or avoid them.

The animals can be transported to locations all over the world by ship, aircraft, or land vehicle. They were used in the Vietnam War and in conflicts in the Middle East.

People have different opinions about the Navy Marine Mammal Program. Some are in favor of the program (pro) and others are against it (con).

Sea lions and dolphins have an **instinct** to hunt under water.

Dolphins have a sense called **echolocation** that allows them to locate objects. A dolphin uses this sense by making clicking sounds, and the sounds bounce off of an object and return, like an echo. Then the dolphin can locate the object. Manmade equipment is not nearly as effective at echolocation as dolphins.

Pro

The Navy Marine Mammal Program should continue because it protects our troops and does not harm marine mammals. Here are three reasons why you should support it.

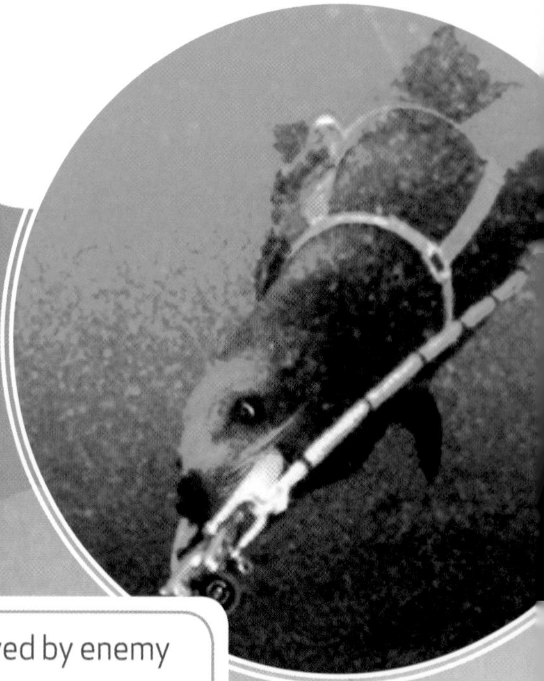

1. First, more ships are damaged or destroyed by enemy sea mines than by any other cause. Dolphins and sea lions locate sea mines and help prevent such disasters, and they do so without touching the sea mines.

2. Secondly, it is unlikely that the animals will be harmed while doing their tasks. Sea mines are designed to be detonated by large ships, not by marine mammals.

3. Finally, the marine mammals are well cared for. The Navy follows the same standards of care as institutions such as the Monterey Bay Aquarium. The animals live in well-maintained enclosures, eat a balanced diet, and have regular exams by a veterinarian.

To protect our troops, we should continue the Navy Marine Mammal Program.

Con

The Navy Marine Mammal Program should not continue because it puts marine mammals at risk. Here are three reasons why you should not support it.

1 First, it's not possible to provide the proper habitat for dolphins in captivity. In nature, dolphins travel up to 50 miles a day in open water. The Navy can't provide this rich habitat because the dolphins live in enclosures except when they are in training or on a mission.

2 Secondly, the capture of dolphins from the wild is harmful. Dolphins live in social groups called *pods*. When they are captured, they are taken away from their pods. Mothers and babies can be separated. Also, some reports say that the chase and capture of dolphins is exhausting and violent.

3 Finally, war is a human problem. Animals are innocent and should not be made to participate. The animals do not choose to join the military as people do. And in the U.S., people have the choice to join or not to join. These animals do not have a choice.

To protect marine mammals, we should end the Navy Marine Mammal Program.

Check In Which opinion do you agree with? Think about and state your reasons.

GENRE Personal Narrative

Read to find out how Harper helps Beth.

One Smart Dog

by Beth Finke

Beth writes in her home office. Harper helps!

I'm blind. Even when my eyes are open, all I see is the color black. So I use my other senses to do things I enjoy, like writing books.

My computer is adapted with assistive technology for people who are blind. A robotic voice parrots the letters I type, and I use my sense of hearing to listen to what I write. When I'm finished with a story, I press a button and . . . *voila!* My computer reads what's on the screen, and I can hear (and fix!) my mistakes.

I do most of my writing at home, but I travel to interview people and research stories. That's where Harper comes in. Harper is my Seeing Eye® dog, and he was specially trained to thread me safely along busy sidewalks and judge traffic at intersections. Harper guides me through crowded airports and anywhere else I need to go.

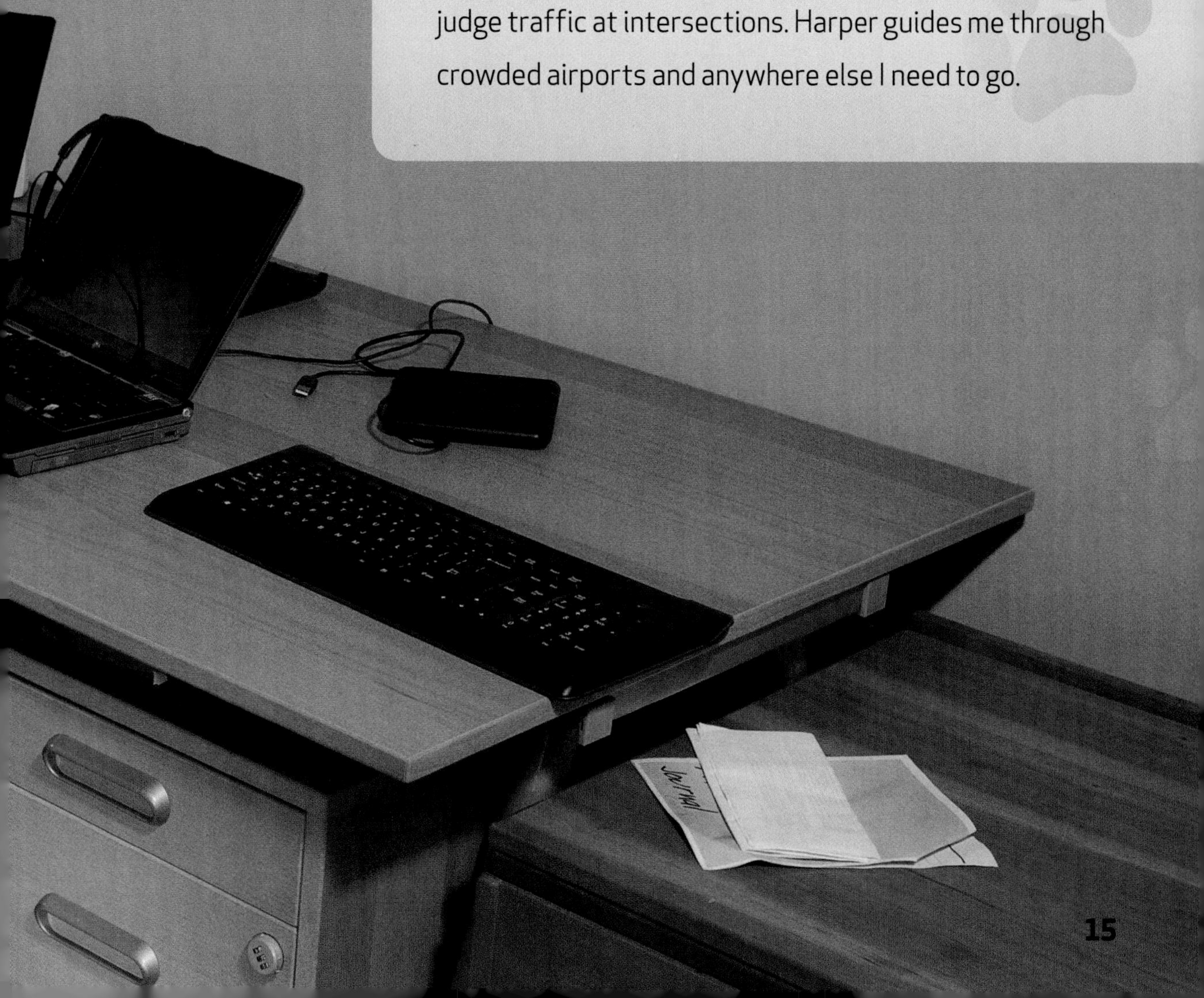

Seeing Eye School in Morristown, New Jersey

Golden Retriever mother and puppies

Harper was trained at the Seeing Eye School , which is the oldest guide dog school in America. Dozens of schools teach guide dogs to help people who are blind, but only dogs trained at the Seeing Eye school earn the official title "Seeing Eye dog." The Seeing Eye school breeds German Shepherds, Golden Retrievers, Labrador Retrievers, and crosses of these breeds. These breeds have **traits** that make them good guide dogs.

When Harper was seven weeks old, he went to live with a volunteer, called a puppy raiser. Harper's puppy raiser taught him the basics: "sit" and "down," normal dog stuff. Puppy raisers can take puppies to places other animals are not allowed. Harper's puppy raiser took Harper everywhere, exposing him to all sorts of people in all sorts of places—crowds at amusement parks, business people rushing to trains, kids splashing in pools.

Puppy raisers must take dogs to crowded places, like baseball games.

After his first birthday, Harper returned to the school. For four long months, professional trainers spent every day reminding Harper to stop at stairs and streets. Harper learned to judge traffic, and he was taught what "left" and "right" and "forward" mean.

Once Harper was ready, I flew to the Seeing Eye school to meet him. I fell in love with this loveable ball of yellow fur the minute I saw (okay, touched!) him. After practicing together for three weeks, I felt confident I could trust Harper to keep me safe in traffic, so it was time to fly home.

Harper's ID card

I feed and take care of Harper, and that's important because it helps build a bond between us. Now every morning I scoop out a cup of dog food, level it with my finger and pour it into Harper's bowl. Harper and I use two pieces of equipment to get around: a harness that buckles around his chest with a sturdy handle for me to grab, and a leash I attach to his collar. Once Harper is done eating, I clip on his leash, buckle his harness and **command,** "Harper, forward!" When we arrive at Harper's favorite tree, I unbuckle his harness so he knows it's okay to empty. (That's a polite word for *pee* and *poop*.)

Back home, I unbuckle Harper's harness and head to the kitchen sink. I lift his water bowl, and if it feels light, I know it's empty. I turn the water on, test the temperature, and fill Harper's bowl until it feels heavy again. I groom Harper every day, and when our workday is over we play tug-of-war and fetch with his favorite toys.

Beth uses a brush to groom Harper.

Harper loves to play.

Harper guides Beth across a street.

Good Dog!

Close your eyes and imagine you can't see. Here's what you'd do to travel down a street with a Seeing Eye dog.

- **Lift the harness handle with your left hand.**
- **Face the direction you want to go.**
- **Say your dog's name and command, "Forward!"**
- **Hold on tight! Your dog will pull you forward.**
- **When your dog stops, you stop, too.**
- **Slide your foot forward to investigate why the dog stopped. Feel a curb, the top of the stairs, a hole in the sidewalk? Praise your dog. He just saved you from falling. "Good dog!"**

Seeing Eye dogs fight their natural **instincts** to chase, scavenge, sniff, protect, and socialize while they're working. Out in the city, if Harper gets distracted by a squirrel zipping by, or a kid dropping an ice cream cone, he might forget to stop at the curb.

And that's just the beginning. We still have to cross the street!

Dogs are color blind, so Harper can't tell if the stoplight is red or green. It's my job to judge when it's safe to cross. I stand up straight, concentrate, and listen for the rush of cars. When it sounds like the traffic is going the direction I want to go, I guess that the light is green. "Harper, forward!" Harper's ears perk up. He listens for traffic and looks left and right to determine whether it's safe to pull me across.

If he thinks I've misjudged the traffic, or if he sees a motorist speeding toward us at the last minute, Harper stays put. I can repeat the command and urge him forward. Doesn't matter. Harper won't budge. Not until he's confident it's safe.

Let me tell you a little about **intelligent disobedience,** or refusing a command that is dangerous. Intelligent disobedience is the most difficult skill a Seeing Eye dog must learn. Harper uses intelligent disobedience at street crossings, and he uses it in other situations, too. I'll leave you with a great example.

Harper and I were heading down a city sidewalk once when he stopped for no reason. Well, no reason that I could come up with.

I felt ahead with my foot. Nothing there. I waved my arm in front of me. No barricade.

"Harper, forward!" I urged. I had an appointment, and I didn't want to be late. "Hup, hup!" Harper stood motionless.

"Right, right!" I tried, hoping Harper might skirt me around whatever he saw in the way. No luck.

Just then I heard a truck door slam. Heavy footsteps hurried toward us. "Watch out, ma'am! Stay put!" The truck driver offered his arm. "They just called me to come fix this door!" He guided us into the street for a bit, then led us back onto the sidewalk. "There's glass all over the place!"

The plate glass door had shattered. I couldn't have known this, but Harper did.

"That's one smart dog," our new friend told me. "Thanks," I agreed, giving Harper a scratch on the head before lifting his harness to continue on our way. "I think so, too!"

Harper watches for obstacles ahead.

That's one smart dog!

Check In How do Harper and Beth work together?

Discuss Text Structure, Details, and Examples

1. Describe how "Animals Can!" is organized. How does the organization help you compare information about the animals?

2. How are the opinions organized in "The Navy Marine Mammal Program"?

3. What reasons and evidence are presented to support the two differing opinions in "The Navy Marine Mammal Program"?

4. Think of an animal that you know, such as a pet. What kind of job would it be suited for? Explain why. Refer to details and examples from "Animals Can!"

5. What do you still wonder about working animals? What more would you like to find out?